What We Have in Common

A Brim Coloring Book

Written by Jane Landey
Edited by David Austin

Drawings by David Austin and Jane Austin

Copyright©2017

All rights reserved.

Published by CreateSpace: An Amazon Company.
Printed in U.S.A.

Introduction

What We Have in Common. Brim Coloring Books enable children color the drawings as they read along! The books display the similarities of related animals. In this series the cat and the owl are compared. The facts enable children to appreciate common values. Thus, imbibing in them interest towards animals which could help them appreciate what they have in common with one another.

The Cat

And

The Owl

A cat and an owl meet under a big tree.

My name is Mister Cat!

I am Mister Owl!

I am one of the many cats in my family.

I am one of the many owls in mine.

I am called Brown Cat.

I am called Great Horned Owl.

I love to meow!

I love to hoot!

I search for rats and mice which are
my favorite food to eat!

Me too!

I catch rats and mice with my
sharp paws.

I catch rats and mice with my sharp claws too!

My round face is lovely!

My round face is adorable to see!

My two ears flip out when they hear
any sound.

My ears can receive many sounds too!

Can you see my shining eyes?

Yes, I can!

I love to walk about in the night.

I love to watch from the tree at night too!

I can jump from the tree.

I Can too when I want to!

Can you climb on a house?

I can fly on top of a house, if I want to.

Do you want to go hunting with me?

Yes, I would love to go with you!

I will call you tomorrow then.

I will answer you then!

Do not be late then!

I won't!

Bye, See you!

Bye!

What We Have in Common Brim Coloring Books

Crocodile and Alligator
Turtle and Tortoise
Starfish and Octopus
Worm and Snake
Turkey and Vulture
Ostrich and Emu
Weka and Kiwi
Bat and Rat
Camel and Llama
Duck and Pelican
Kangaroo and Wallaby
Pig and Tapir
Skunk and Squirrel
Hedge and Anteater
Cat and Owl
Elephant and Rhinoceros
Dog and Fox
Buffalo and Bull
Leopard and Cheetah
Horse and Zebra